WHISTLE MAKER

Robert J. Levy

Anhinga Press
Tallahassee, Florida

ISBN 0—938078—22—4
ISBN 0—938078—23—2

FIRST EDITION

Published by Anhinga Press, Tallahassee, Florida
Cover art by Peter Elwell

ACKNOWLEDGEMENTS

Boulevard: "The Actress"
Chelsea: "On the Pythagorean Theorem"
Georgia Review: "Whistle Maker," "American Country"
Kayak: "Winter Rain," "King Kong, Married," "Window Dressing," "Give Us This Day Our Daily Day," "Noun Gathering at Dusk," "The Don of Toast," "Thanks," "To a Fly Trapped in Amber"
Michigan Quarterly Review: "Sestina: Perrier"
Outerbridge: "The Tristan Chord," "The English Garden"
Poetry Now: "Late One Night"
Poetry Society of America Bulletin: "Gettysburg," "Kuli Loach"
Prairie Schooner: "The Healing"
Quarterly West: "The Country of Enumerability"
River Styx: "Hiatus"
Seneca Review: "Kappa"
Sonora Review: "On Style," "Buffalo Abstract"
Stone Country: "Waiting for Snow"
Yankee: "Horse and Writer"

"Give Us This Day Our Daily Day," "Winter Rain," and "Waiting for Snow" have been reprinted, respectively, in the 1981, 1984, and 1985 editions of *Anthology of Magazine Verse & Yearbook of Poetry*

"The Tristan Chord," "The Healing," "Worm," "Fish," "The Tackle Box," "Kappa," "Window Dressing," "Give Us This Day Our Daily Day," "American Country," "The Country of Enumerability," "Sestina: Perrier," "Buffalo Abstract," "Kuli Loach," "To a Fly Trapped in Amber," and "Whistle Maker" appeared in *The Glitter Bait,* a chapbook of poems published by the Arts-Wayland Foundation in 1986.

for Kari, again

CONTENTS

I

II

III

I

Melting Pot

Here is a leek, a vegetable my grandmother
has probably never heard of, much less tasted,
but each time I make *poule au pot* I think of her
and of the distance I have come to be cooking
something she'd refer to as "*goyishe* onions."
"French schmench," she'd say, "a chicken is a chicken."

Could I tell her she was wrong, that sometimes even
the lowliest fowl is transmogrified, and a bird
of humble origins may, with perseverance,
fly far from a *shtetl* in Galicia up to
Manhattan's smart West Side without dropping
a pinfeather? No, she'd tell me about chickens,

about all those slaughtered in *der alte heym*
and how each beheading was a joy and loss
as palpable as one's own flesh. She'd say
each chicken has but one life to give, that it must
be used advisedly but simply as the Lord
would have it—koshered, hung until the blood has drained—

and then it must be "boiled," not "simmered" as my sort
would tend to do. How else to draw the flavor out
into the broth? After all the meat had been
consumed, she'd drop root vegetables into the stock—
parsnips, turnips—things that grow beneath the soil
to remind us how a chicken comes full circle

for our people, how what is sweet in life must turn
bitter so we won't forget our origins
in suffering and pain, forget the earthen taste
of our beginnings in a thousand ghettos
whose names are unpronounceable. She'd tell me
I am a fool who has read too many books

for his own good and that history moves through us
like disease—or nourishment—and no matter
where I run I'll never run quite far enough away.
Still, I have come this far. Tonight, I make a meal
of *poule au pot*. It is delicious and liberating.
It is boiled chicken by another name.

Gadrooned Edge

Because it is perfect and unassailable,
swirled purple with a haze of Nordic blue,
the vase you moved beneath the palm
seems suddenly as apt and elegant
as an equation of the beautiful,
and because it is lovely, I can love you
for teaching me devotion to the frill,
the fillip and the furbelow.

Believe me, this is not the casual,
offhanded praise a man bestows
upon a wife whose detailed attentions
he finds "utterly endearing."
This is philosophy and tears.
It is not the essences of things
but the circumferences that drive
us forward every day—the motes of thought,
wild decorations of belief, ideas
to dance around—and, should we starve ourselves
from all the mind's variety,
we would wither like a noun unadjectived.

This vase, my love, this vase is the ocean
and the coast of Norway, the icy *fjell*
that overlooks a glacial ridge, the thorn
behind which hides an elk, his nostrils flared,
eyes brimming with attack and, distantly,
the white tip of a sail is seen receding
past the furthest rim of sight.

And even if there were an ideal vase
in the vault of the mind—neither
blistered, glazed nor etched with wild design,
sitting squarely on a pedestal of stone,
white, immaculate and utterly alone

in the sepulchre of thought—still, we would not
wish it in our scene, because perfection,
here, in all our moments,
is always momentary at the best.

Your placing of this vase is wonderful:
I can conjure up no higher praise.
We are only as permanent
and beautiful as we decide to be.
Though all our days are but a dress-up game
in self-created finery, we sail
the edge of things and circumnavigate
the far sublime in search of treasures
from a heaven we will never see. Love,
let us go together in our little boat.

In Sickness

Three weeks married to our symptoms
and no change in sight. Hot flashes
baffle us by day. Sudden chills
confuse us through the night. Even
sickness, however, can begin
to look like health in time, and ours,
despite its fever sweats and rheums,
has become domesticated
to a pattern of remissions,
always brief, that allows us both
to spell the other for awhile
before the next attack begins.

Monday you read me Baudelaire
in bed. Tuesday it is my turn
to bring you *meusli* and a peach.
As the days wear on we trade off
the thermometer between us
like an Olympian's baton:
We run our relay race to see
who can take care of whom the best
and for how long. We just can't do
enough for each other. Frankly,
all this fevered giving becomes
quite tiresome after three weeks

sick in bed, and soon we feign all
our infirmities—withered hands,
a vile catarrh . . . anything to
inject a little selfishness
into our lives. What parity
there is in marriage and disease
is slowly weakened to the point
of no return. Still, we are left

much less alone somehow, in love
once more with the mundanity
of being well, having returned,
at long last, to our chronic norm.

Precision

The sky is so glazed and dreamy
with approaching storm a white seagull
redefines the air it moves through
like a paintbrush—a stark swath of contrast
splayed across a black surround. We too want
this precision, you and I—the detail
that liberates and sets the world ablaze.

Always we strive for it, for anything
that might have wings. Last night I spoke to you
by phone. In your voice was that gaiety
I have come to know as the cutting edge
of hysteria. Rehearsals, you said,
were going well enough, but weren't sure.
I replied, the writing's coming fine.

When we hung up we knew no more
about each other than before we called.
We had our work, and our work moved
through us like a lover—bitchy,
half the time in heat, and always
more exacting and demanding
than the time before. As in a failed

ménage à trois we bed down each night with
a specific beauty in hopes
of waking with the beautiful. It seems
we always wake alone. Today I rose
to the cries of seagulls buoyed
in from off the bay, their voices
meaningless as our words last night. I went

down to the water where the rain
was preparing its black masterpiece.
The gull wheeled against the dark horizon,

eloquent as a perfect, chosen word,
and then sheered out of sight. Tonight
I will call you again. I will tell you
about the sky and the seagull,

about how, together for one instant,
there was neither bird nor backdrop
but something so complete it seemed
to burn against the sky. I will tell you
how they comprised a world, how, when the air
finally cleared, the seagull departed
leaving one white feather on the water.

The Tristan Chord

More alone with this music than ever before
I find myself thinking of you,
of that other loneliness, and of how
you always had the words for everything,
the way you once called a Beethoven quartet
"the scraping of horses' tails on cats' bowels."

No doubt you could have
talked a rainbow into grayness.
How many times have you walked out from the opera
humming arias like souvenirs?
What you take away with you is candy:
deliciously oblique and self-contained,

a thing that comforts by confining music
to the boundaries of conversation.
But if you would only listen, quietly,
you would hear. . .nothing.
Not music but music's aspiration
to a silence so complete

whatever you might say about it
would be, pathetically, about yourself.
This is the Tristan chord. It melts
like ice in the palm of a word.
Like a shell's susurrus, it sings
of where it came from, where it's going,

but not of what it is. And where do you
fit into all of this? You don't.
You never did. And that's the core of it.
I could tell you how your words have broadened
my experience of art, of life, etc. . . .
They haven't changed a thing. Lately,

I find myself rehearsing the Tristan chord
in all its variations. I've been thinking
how you and I are like two notes
upon a stave, parts of a tune
but not ourselves a tune. I've been thinking how words
escape us—or we from them. I've been thinking

that the search for cadence takes a very long time.

Gettysburg

Winds are petitioning the masonry
for answers here on Seminary Ridge.
Further out, the hills are soft with fog.
The road we walk is new. It winds through both.
Once, following that gleaming stretch
of macadam into the battlefields,
we found someone had cleaned the past
and labeled it, and called it "history."
The signs said, "On this spot died so and so. . ."
and it was fact. Things attested to it.
Cannon eyed the scene like statuary.
Pyramids of shot were heaped like little graves.
One time we drove out to Little Round Top
and found a boulder that spoke perfect English:
Press a button and it explains who died
right where you stand. When we drove back it was
silently, through fog, along the forest road.
It was all very strange. Too strange, perhaps,
to be sad. After, the seminary
seemed almost real. We could find no headstones
with engraved assurance that, "He rose here,
here in Gettysburg, on this very hill. . ."
Everything was as silent as the chapel
which stood like a monument to someone
expected and unnamed, remembered
and unknown. Bloated leaves depended
from thin trees, stuttered slightly in the breeze
but did not fall. That day I think we realized
uncertainty, as well, may be a passion
here in Gettysburg, where tourists
and theologians wait for miracles
to happen, for those that happened,
those that might, and those that never will,
and the wind knocking on the doors of stones,
and the level fog rolling up the ridge. . . .

Waiting for Snow

Snow in New York is unlike snow
in any other place. Days now
we've been waiting, the air itself
petulant with cold, our noses

etching clear question marks along
glazed windowpanes. Still, nothing happens.
The belly of the sky grows fat
with northern promises and we,

made weary by the weather man
and all his inklings, disbelieve
in any but real presences.
We go on waiting for the snow

even though when, at last, it comes,
we will not see the drifts collect
from this fifteenth floor apartment
without a view. Snow will not change

a thing for us, any more than strange
tales of other snows from ages past.
Nothing happens. So we go on
waiting for the world to don its cassock

and perform the winter liturgy
in which each snowflake is distinct, the same
story told anew each time, pure, unreal,
so white it has to be believed.

Winter Rain

My friend in Warsaw writes to me of rain, of the different types of Polish rain—the filthy spray, the crystal mist, the warm, fat droplets souring the earth—and of how this winter there will be no winter by an order of the state. A continuance of autumn has been declared. His letters mention endless names of towns—a glottal litany, all consonant, that stumbles off the tongue—and how unrest mounts incrementally, like water rising in a rain gauge. He writes of how he spends whole days refusing visas to potential emigrants who spend as many days inventing nonexistent jobs and relatives awaiting them across the sea. And through all of this—the knowing glances of the men who tail him everywhere he goes, the card games in the dungeon of the embassy, the hushed exchange of dying currency for lethal dollars—there is the rain as agent of the state, which forbids the sweet release from autumn into snow. Now I must write back to him. I feel I should say something profound about survival in a foreign land, about the intransigence of freedom when it's held in chains, about all rain being relative and how he must, at last, remain aloof and cold. I tear up a first draft, then a second, then a third as each revision starts to seem redundant and obscene. And then, another letter comes by mail. In it my friend reports the snows have come at last, bringing with them much public celebration and drinking of cold vodka. At last I come to know my jealousy, my envy of a land so grim and strange. I look out my window at the whiteness blanketing New York and begin a letter to my friend in Warsaw, "Dear George, snow, in a free country, is only snow . . ."

The Healing

On the night his sister almost died
of spinal meningitis, there by her bed
was the blue *Science & Health* her spastic
fingers toyed with like a talisman,

and there he was fetching her water,
joking, acting almost like a brother,
coercing laughter from between the screams
as the dark creature strummed her spine.

Every night it would be the same:
mother in the kitchen praying, the screams
growing worse, father lying in bed
and turning up the T.V. very loud,

and he remembers thinking at times
how comic, because so laughably extreme.
That night, black men in white took her away
to the hospital. Families are crazy.

Father stayed on. Mother clung with new life
to the clean, dead bird of her faith.
He retired to his room for seven years,
a bit out of sorts, packing his gear

and perusing the brochures. He left as he came:
an eccentric guest, cordially thanking them
for the clean sheets and meals. He closed the door
behind him like the amen in a prayer.

Worm

Dazzled among grassroots I inch
far from the rarefied half-world
of leaf mold and mushroom tuft.
I drill into the denser loam
that parts before me like great waves
of primal clay. This is gorgeous
swimming. To veer round a pebble
is a sacrament of the soil.
I go down, down. Sometimes across.
It doesn't matter. Perfection
is where my guts happen to be
at each moment. Dirt is my den,
reeking corruption's sweet perfume—
the potpourris of old manure.
Fragrant weed-rot simmers behind
the nearest stone. Death's delicious,
itself a kind of worm that churns
the unencumbered dross of earth
into new fruit. So damn the mole,
the shrew, the wren—the killer things
that clutch and catch. Nothing slows me.
Not the choking rain, the chafing
drought. Not the heavy surface plod
of wheels and feet. I just go on
in my element—down, across—
ready for that final nudging
when the segments slow, cilia
furl against the flesh, and brightness,
incredible brightness, conquers
all—a sort of celebration,
like being at last welcomed home
by myself as I truly am.

Fish

I would be a trout for you if I could,
down here in the silver-cool,
barely breathing beneath a lilypad,
a mere ripple in the corner of your eye.

All day I pray for your line,
tricked out with candy,
to be offered to my lips. All day
I've sweated air, waiting, waiting.

To get your attention
I strike the ceiling like a knife,
right through the mayfly's heart,
and leap into your empty creel.

Does this grab your eye? Must I sing
or fly? What is it, though, the worm
writhing so sweetly before me,
that folds my fins before the strike?

It shines! In the worm's brain it shines!
So. You would hit me on the head.
You would eat me. You would have me stuffed
and stuck above your mantelpiece.

It is not as I thought.
It's lonely down here in the silver-cool,
but there's shrimpy things for company,
and sometimes, when it rains,

I leap up so high it's like
taking a long drink of heaven.
Did I mention I saw you recently
floating by in the flatbottom?

Like a faraway cloud you blocked
the sun, so busy drowning worms
you failed to notice me there:
the big one that got away.

The Tackle Box

A three-tiered candy case of barbed
mutations, it wintered in the cupboard
till those summer mornings
we plied the Ramapo
for pickerel. Gun-metal blue,
rimed with orange rust from when Dad
threw it overboard, it doubled
as my hope chest those long, hot days
spent angling for his affections.
As guardian of bait, it was
up to me to choose the lures—
spinners, plugs and jigs. Mornings
we always started out with "spoons"—
flat, teardrop shards of polished steel
that hugged the bottom muck for bass
or weeds. It happened early on:
Enraged by the fishes' tight-lipped
refusal to bite, he grew mute
and edgy with failure. I then
began the ritual exchange,
first offering a Jitterbug—
a plough-mouthed, stylized cockroach
he trolled for a while until
it snagged a lilypad. To calm
him down I tried the rubber-skirted
Hula Popper, propeller-nosed
sardines, electric silverfish
that sent out ultrasonic radar blips.
Technology failed. Next he tried
live bait: bloodsucker worms, turgid
purple muscles he desperately
impaled on hooks. The trout
just stole them for hors d'oeuvres.
By late afternoon he said
I'd scared off all the fish,

then he punched me in the arm
and made me row to shore. Climbing into
the car, he swore never to take
me anywhere again. Silent
in the back seat, I was
something thrown back in the stream—
too small but no less hooked for that.
I held the tackle box, imagining
all those sharp delicacies.

The English Garden

When I first saw the English garden
it was mown scant as a putting green,
bound around its periphery
by whatever living filigree might grow,
and there you were, weeding and pruning.

It seemed a pleasant sort of place.
Lilacs in early spring, then mums
and roses, and towards fall, a bumper crop
of ridiculous potatoes.
I took up residence in the English garden.

You served me tea in the English garden,
with rich cakes, exotic loaves and fresh preserves.
But I could barely touch a crumb,
so filled was I with your loveliness.

Late one summer, having reached my green majority,
I left the English garden.
I can still see you with your shears in hand.
Tears, like admonitions, wavered on your cheek
as you engaged your lonely task.

I traveled widely in the intervening years,
pursuing the oblique and strange.
On my return voyage I was wondering
how things were with you and the English garden.

And there you were, almost as I had left you,
lovely, though the English garden
seemed to wilt about you and a wisp
of cobweb traced itself across your cheek.

We were married that fall.
It was a simple ceremony—you, me

and the English garden presiding.
Then we left that country for the final time.

Now we have planted an English garden
here in America. It is not so nice
nor quite so self-contained as its original
but it will serve.

You have become old.
You have become beautiful.
We never have elaborate parties.

In the American version
of the English garden
tea is what we do to keep us warm.

King Kong, Married

You placed her on a pedestal
for all to see. Remember how
the papers sported photos of you
flagging biplanes down, insouciantly,
shouting your love to the whole city.

Back then, when your whirlwind courtship
captured the public's jaded eye,
you gave no thought for the future.
Today, things are different. New York
changes one in hardly subtle ways.

Now you have a wife who drinks beer,
reads French novels, scans recipes
you know she won't prepare—attractive
in an ugly sort of way, she greets you
every night with wet-eyed adulation.

Weekends she sits darning a sock
draped like a flag across her knees
while your underwear billows sail-like
on the fire escape. None the less
an enervating *joie de vivre*

suffuses everything you do.
You come home after a workday
that would have toppled smaller men
with "plans for the evening." You swim,
you paint, you sing, take dance lessons. . .

But let's be honest. You're unhappy
with your life and these words are merely
mollification for a giant
who put his love up on the highest pedestal
of all, only to discover

it was getting there that mattered,
that it might have been better to fall
than climb down into what you have become.
Those front-page photos should have told you—
next to a giant, she really looks quite small.

Heat Lightning

On these barren evenings, waiting for rain,
I often calculate a storm's approach
by reckoning the time elapsed between
lightning and thunder. It's one way
to avoid thoughts of other distances,

of how, behind the constant flash of words
from some long-familiar face, one sometimes
hears a rumbling that would go unnoticed
but for a slight shift in the direction
of conversation and a clouding of the eyes.

Many times I have wished for an algebra
to make you explode in tears or laughter
at the end of some long, drawn-out avoidance
of our love. But often as not
I miscalculated. You were never

the sort to yield to numbers and their plans.
You moved through weathers that were yours alone:
ground fogs lit by an unearthly glow,
clear mornings indecipherable from night.
Even your leaving was unpredicted,

a quiet dispersal of energies
more than decisiveness. The winds took you
or you let yourself be blown. Tonight,
heat lightning has been scissoring
the sky for hours while thunder booms

relentlessly beyond the hills. There are
no numbers I can wedge between
the flash and noise, no formula
to hold a woman to her promising
or enchant a storm from nothing.

Sheep

Jammed nose to tail, the ewes and rams
approach in pairs, gingerly at first,
then with more bravado when they see
our hands deep in our pockets. Bleating

plaintively, their black-mask faces
comical and mute as question marks,
they've come for food. It was four years ago
that we first surprised them

near a cul-de-sac behind the graves.
They stumbled clumsily on thin legs stiff
as stilts, nuzzling against us, refusing
to believe our hands were bare of grain.

The year after, no longer ingenues,
they tried licking and cajoling barley
from our empty palms, stamping angrily
when they found our soft caresses would not

nourish them. Jaded by our touch,
they wandered off beyond the rise.
Last time was difficult for both of us:
We barely made it back. Blizzard burned

the meadow with a sugar crust of snow.
Dripping icicles of snot, they
took reluctant steps in our direction
then sagged together near the barn for warmth.

This year, fear is foremost in their minds.
Unbelief bites like a leash
into their necks and holds them back,
their hoofbeats staccato and unsure.

Clinging close to each other, they approach
until they see, again, we have no food.
They turn and run, though still in pairs,
their stampede down the slope as resolute

and mutual as their approach. You turn
to me. Let's follow them, you say.
We climb the fence, not bothered
by the splinters punishing our hands.

II

Hiatus

Peeling an orange you realize you've been
thinking no thoughts at all for two minutes,
that the strange ball rotating silently
beneath your hand, shedding its skin in rich
and fragrant coils, is suddenly something
for which you have no name. Try as you will
there's no way of speaking all the quiet
it throws back at you. In that brief moment
you are the action of peeling the fruit
and nothing else, so lost, so utterly
unhinged that, afterwards, you cannot say
what brought you back, what reflex made you breathe
the absolute perfume that wrote the name
of "orange" on your tongue once more. Like a
tired mountain climber returning from an
eminence whose height he can only hope
to comprehend in retrospect, you have
seen all the fruits of your labor reduced
to rind. The small, concave valleys of peel
litter the table where you stand. They held
something once, something that was called "orange"
long before the universe revolved you
slowly in its hands, paring you away.

Kappa

Here is Shoko's pouting Kappa—
a *netsuke* carved from boxwood
in the mid-nineteenth century.

He has reduced the dimensions
of a myth to something smaller
than a thumb, and even less severe.

Notice the plaintive, childlike
upturning of the face and eyes,
and recall the legend of the beast—
its penchant for drowning wayfarers
unless mollified with cucumbers.

The saucer-shaped depression
in its skull contained a fluid
making it uncompromising
and ferocious.
                    Remember, though,
its downfall was gentility—
being Japanese, whenever
bowed to it would bow politely
in reply, spilling the liquid
and so losing all its strength.

Notice how the ears peek coyly
from the sharp striations of the hair
to reaffirm its boyish charm,
but most of all, see how the artist
tamed a creature of the mind's
imagining and brought it home
to rest once more.
                    Note, finally,
how its full-bodied realism

allows perusal from all sides.

The Japanese have a word for this—
katabori, which simply means
the artist has left no surface untouched.

Horse and Writer

From the nightmare stable
horses wake to gelid air
and race along the strand's
absurd expanse of white
in search of equipoise.

Their trail is like a pen's stroke
on a page. It tells us
animals have been here,
that everything is changed
to oddments thrown up
as if by chance along
the water's edge—scallop shells
like shattered teacups, pale
gratuities of sand dollars,
a squid's last letter inked
upon the beach where
a hermit crab, unhoused,
endures his naked world alone.
As with dreams, the strangest things
resolve to something known.

No one owns these horses.
They return the shore into
a thing of their own making,
vaguely human, with a sound
of rampant surf like whispered
conversation—our voices
given back to us more strange.
They dissolve into the mind
that made them. They revise us
back into the world again.

Window Dressing

A window is whatever's made of it
by chance. The blond girl stripping off her clothes
next door has just been framed, legitimized
somehow, by fortuitous location
and a sudden breeze.

The muslin drapes and morning light are swept
into a fine distraction, and the jar
of potpourri upon the window sill,
the peacock feather in the vase below
her arm, all mingle

there to give larger meaning to the word
"exquisite." Nothing pornographic here
to charm a voyeur's fantasy, nothing
even vaguely sexual. There's too much
balancing of parts.

The girl's as much a still-life as the jar
of French cologne. The peacock plume's as much
a portrait as the girl. The window waits
as always for the universe to pass
before it in review.

The girl puts on her dress and leaves. Something
different takes her place, complete with feather,
drapes, cologne and potpourri. The window
is unchanged. It is always fully clothed,
naked to the world.

Give Us This Day Our Daily Day

Some things are blessedly alyrical.
A stone, immobile in its rut,
is not a poem. A weed does not sing
but for a random fingering of wind.
The tree just hunkers down, a green fact.

The failed poetry of our intentions
is like this. The rhythms lag to a walk.
The fine threads unravel from the yarn.
We find ourselves beautifully entangled
in the unwinding prose of our days.

American Country

In the folk art musuem
the visitors are like wheat
looking at pictures of wheat.

A new crop springs up every few minutes,
craning for a peek
at tolework or fraktur,

only to be mown down
by a glimpse of quilts
or decoys far across the room.

Should a patchwork cow
devour them, or a painting
of a field return them to

the holy, golden city
of their dreams,
they would still pass.

Like the weather vane
in its glass case,
patinaed from a hundred years

of giving directions,
they no longer need to know
which way the wind is blowing.

The Actress

Ask the tear to play a raindrop—
it will leap off the lash for you.

Ask the actress to make you cry.
She will not undergo sea-change,

her molecules rearranging
to the tragic mode. Instead she'll

find a language of least gesture
for sorrow in which the movement

that she makes appears to be
the only motion possible.

Like a coy lover she has teased
a tear from the eye of the man

in the first row. He is moved by
the beauty of her death, but more

so by the beauty of her breasts,
which press against the thin fabric

of her gown like small animals.
He wants to sleep with her after

the show. He wants to sleep with her
now, before the curtain falls.

The actress thinks she's failed her art—
her body's rough vitality

upstaging her, the young man's heat
melting the costume from her flesh.

But is the tear less genuine
for that? The man will never sleep

with her. The actress will never
die. These are things to cry about.

The curtain descends. The applause
comes like a sudden fall of rain.

Noun Gathering at Dusk

A lisp of grass, a slur of wind. . .
soft language from the blackened verge
of wood. I am noun gathering
at dusk. It is dying autumn,
cold season of the nominal
when drowsy words go foraging
for winter homes. With no field guide
but instinctive music, one must
move cautiously over such space
as names allow at night, learning
their migrations by listening
to the wind the mind makes searching
in the dark. A net of meanings
is the only tool required
in pursuit, for they are neither
arch nor devious but simple
ingenues of clear intention
in the modifying forest.
Tonight, they light on every thought
with equanimity. Their joy
consists of falling into snares
of connotation, gradually
becoming tangled in the wet
revivifying grace of words.
Once captured, they must be possessed
and loved completely, as only
self-created things can be.
The sweet and sanctifying greed
of our delight will chasten them.
Imprisoned in our cages
they will shine on us forever,
shine more brightly for being ours.

The Country of Enumerability

for R.W.J.

How we can say "this, and this, and then this"
amazes time and again. The objects
dart their minnow glance at us, swimming up
into the glitter bait within our eyes,

until they're trapped and made more beautiful
inside the mind. So it goes in this place—
whether pedestrian, exotical
or derby-dark, the world's variety

of color, shape and noise is made by us
and fed to bursting with our love. Nothing
cerulean is alien to us,
nothing so dun or drab it can't be fashioned

in the makeshift framework of a phrase
or cordoned off in song. We don't create
the world but its diversity. Our act
of naming is a pure enchantment

and the flattering of everything
into a place it can call "home." Sometimes
it happens unannounced. The sun flames red
toward evening, scars the clouds with mystery. . .

meanwhile the jaded eye rejects the show
and gives itself to driftwood, clapboard huts
and sand, to be finally collected,
mingled by the brash young finger-painter

hidden deep within our souls. Steamy
evenings, when absence is the visible
alternative to light, the world goes blank

and virginal once more, a blackboard

hung with stars for all our good behavior.
Nothing here is dark forever, nothing
so dreary it cannot be regaled
with laying on of hands and with our love.

In the land of enumerability
something is always shining—a ray, a spark,
a glimmer from the eyelid's dewy edge
where the sun is eternally rising.

III

The Sports Pages

We read them with such diligence—
that last reserve of macho grunt and grind
where everyone who sweats can be "all right,"
where stats and stamina are the index
of a partial, mitigating grace
in which the body tries outdistancing
the body's inclinations to surcease.

There are those duffers who would have you think
that there is nothing in it but the glitter
of the names and salaries, all blaring
from the headlines like a vulgar, glossy
neon-lit marquee. In all the action
they see nothing but an instant replay
of their jealousy—those arms and torsos
twice as thick and lithe as theirs.

Some will tell you it provides examples
for the errant young of excellence
or that it is pure, "American,"
and some still promulgate the lie
of male fraternity, of how, in sport,
all men are brothers in a world of men.
Even commercials chant the litany—
going the distance, grabbing the gusto,
playing one more set for that icy can
of brew, reaching deep inside for that last
expression of the masculine sublime
until, finally, something in the mind,
some rooting section in the mezzanine,
calls out for "Deee-fense! Deee-fense!" as the clock
starts winding down, and you know, at last,
that none of these are explanations
for the whole, but mere addenda
to presumptive understanding.

Perhaps it's something to do with the won/lost
column that grabs us by the throat, the way
they head out every day onto the court,
the field, the rink and come home every night
with something that's objective, crystalline,
a debit or a credit in their lives.

We eat. We drink. We sleep. We tell ourselves
that we are good—not *very* good,
but passable, and friendly to a fault.
But still, our wives don't greet us at the door
in negligees or take their panties off
in public places. And our secretaries
surely don't. Our bosses never slap us
on the ass announcing "Job well done!"
as though we'd just pitched three flawless innings
of relief at Ebbets Field.

So we hunger, and are not satisfied,
and grow more hungry every day
for life that's lived in increments—
not those of minutes, days, financial years,
but quarters, rounds and halves, those periods
of hot decision where each step
we take will matter in the end.

We don't *read* the sports pages. We *eat* them.
We make of them a meal which, once inside,
ennobles us, expands us, so that when
we step up to the plate of our desires
(pathetic, magnificent) and hear the roar,
and point out towards the left-field bleachers
while a young boy listens from his sick-bed
at the state infirmary, we know,
for all time and for all places,
exactly where that ball will go.

Sestina: Perrier

We savor all that is most dear to us—water
for example—and render it sublime
through apotheosis. Green, tear-shaped bottles
plague our cupboards with refreshment. Of pure thirst
we know little save the natural
desire, after jogging, for a cool drink.

Neither too cloying nor too sweet, what we drink
is really pure potential. As water
slithers from the tap—cloudy, incorrect, unnatural—
we reject it as obscene, sublimate
our gray despair at what we are, our thirst
for what we want to be. So we bottle

it in something beautiful. We bottle
it because there is no other way to drink
and still keep sane. Though we might sometimes thirst
for cola, aquavit or lemonade, it's water
we return to, sparkling water with its sublime
promise that we will be one with nature

in the end, that if our drink is pure and natural
we too will become pure. Pale, verdant bottles
beckon to us, suggesting some sublime
mountain freshet a traveler would gladly drink
his last from. So when we take such water
we sip the ocean of our choice, quench a thirst

beyond mere need for liquid sustenance, a thirst
for what we'd like to be, where our natural
environment is tennis courts and freshly watered
lawns, and on the sideboard . . . salmon mousse, gay bottles
in a row. Hope is our aperitif. We drink
the future like a dream of the sublime

until, one day, something subliminal
warns us of the futility of thirst,
that though we are what we eat, we drink
all we are hoping to become. It's our nature
to be forlorn. So we take to the bottle.
We find no rejuvenation in sparkling water.

What was sublime this morning grows unnatural
by noon. Our thirst becomes too big for any bottle.
We all forget why we ever drank our water.

On Style

Moët Chandon and Brie de Meaux
have graced your table many times,
but not till tonight did I learn
the ratio between how poor
you were and how lavishly you lived.
Style, you said, transcends starvation—
only part jest. I can attest
to the abyss of your icebox,
the frozen oddments mired in frost,
putrid heads of lettuce shattered
like a sad, vegetable schrapnel,
a carpet of organic dross
so deep perhaps coal will form there
in a million years. But for now,
miraculously, you survive
on antique crystal, linens
and a nonexistent income,
fashioning from such scraps a world
called comfort in which, though not proud
to be bourgeois, you're not ashamed.
You're the perfect snob. Still, even I can
enjoy the cool, ridiculous
harmony of these plaster chips
falling, like manna, from the ceiling
onto your brand-new Limoges plate.

Late One Night

It was late one night and getting later
when suddenly the T.V. just took off
and began rampaging around the room
like a rabid water buffalo
intent on smashing everything, itself
and us, in its headlong dash from the foyer.
First, like most members of our family,
it charged into the kitchen, opening
the fridge and throwing food on the floor
uneaten, even though there were people
starving in Asia. It pasted cold cuts
all over the walls and ceiling.
Then it really went mad, scratching the baseboards,
tearing contact paper from the cupboards.
We finally cornered it. Exhausted,
cringing with its one huge Cyclopean
eye, it gleamed coldly at us from behind
the pre-amp. We punished it severely.
It has since punished us. The vertical hold
has become willful. If we switch on the news
it shows us "I Love Lucy" or old films
that end too late for us to be awake.
One might say the situation has become
a bit uncomfortable, and sometimes
it turns glassy, ominous and gray,
so gray that you can almost see your face.

The Don of Toast

At an Oxford college a certain don took two slices of toast away with him from breakfast each morning. When he died, forty years worth of toast was found in his room.

One's days are made filthy with rain
and calendar fatigue.
Some embellishments are needed.
As if the years were curios
I've shored up increments of life.
They make compulsive reading.

I can trace my history
in sliced loaves retreating
to a fine oblivion
of dust and vintage marmalade—
the thousand teas with freshers
flushed and shaken from the cold.

Insanity, I've found, is a state of mind
that doesn't go away.
Now I have gone away, leaving nothing.
Like a tattered palimpsest
these stale notes
are written in a buried hand.

No one need learn the reasons
for so perverse a greed.
No one need ever know those nights
I tallied up my past and,
completely happy, calculated
how much butter I would need.

Thanks

Six reindeer on a field of russet wool
forage for the third dimension
in their lives. They nose among patinaed
silver buttons, scavenge lint

and motes of color from their linear
surround. It is a silent world.
No hawk or rook to crack the wilderness
with cries. No lean, unsuspected

predator whose footpad snaps a bramble,
hotly in pursuit. Only reindeer,
red, and chevrons stitched into the landscape,
deltas of a grayish fabric

that are not sleet or snow or anything
in nature, but a slack reality
grown weary of pretense, condensed
into a drear, accusing rain.

Somehow, they have survived the blackest nights
of closeting. Hot summers sealed
in mothballs, packed in cedar chests,
are nothing to them. Such great beasts

are noble and forever. They will race
about this landscape till their threads
grow weary and, like flesh, unravel to
a softer, plusher heaven. By the way,

thanks for this lovely handmade sweater,
and forgive my sentimental
confusion. You see, this is the first time
my clothing has worn animals.

Buffalo Abstract

There's not a buffalo in sight.
Still, one could pray for something wild
barreling blindly down Main Street,
tearing up the pavement (or what
is left of it)—rabid, steaming
like those locomotives that once
fanned out from here, tentacular,
to hug New York's fat, green expanse
within their northerly embrace.
Sunday, downtown is deserted
in this second largest city
of our state. A small buffalo—
all hair and heat and heavy breath—
would be welcome, or a big dog
scrounging chicken wings in doorways.
A minor cat would be relief
and not at all obscene. Any
random animal would do. But
no buffalos, no cows, no goats—
just one lone kid in too-tight jeans
who sidles up to me and asks
for cigarettes. "Fresh out," I say.
But no one is "fresh" out up here—
they've either got it or they
haven't had it for a long, long time.
"You wanna buy some hash?" he asks.
I shake my head, moving along.
Behind me is the sound of hooves.

On the Pythagorean Theorem

If we listen to those who wish to recount ancient history, we may find some of them referring this theorem to Pythagoras and saying that he sacrificed a brace of oxen in honor of his discovery.

from Proclus

Just as a bell curve is a kind
of breast with meaning, or graphed
hyperbolae can represent
the coy geometry of lust
(the soft curves of infinite approach
and loss), so too I can believe
that when Pythagoras deduced
the theorem, his sacrifice of
oxen to the gods was not
prompted by piety alone.

Was it for the sake of gods
the dumb beasts were spitted, charred and sent
ethereal, to bovine heaven?
Did he believe the theorem had descended,
courtesy of some mathematical
Prometheus, from on high?

I would like, instead, to think
that the electric "click" of certainty,
flooding his mind like light into a room
where only dark had been before,
was like the voice of a lovely woman
reclaiming him into the world.

At once abstract and visceral,
the "ah ha!" of sudden knowing
was like the "ahhh . . ." of sexual release,
and knowledge struck the belly of his mind

with the neat certainty of wine.

I would like to think he understood
that truth was not otherworldly,
that a fact may reek of burning meat
and its proper offering must be
the smoke from flesh on fire, the smell
of food and sex, the aroma
(corrupt, delicious) of knowledge—
the smoldering thigh pieces of the beast.

Kuli Loach

Witness to the guppy wars
and countless couplings
of gouramis, he had earned
my grudging admiration
by being what he was
and nothing more. Scavenger,
voyeur, devourer of snail turds,
algae and the more glamorous
droppings of the angelfish,
he slipped along the gravel
of my aquarium like memory,
consuming all the refuse
of the present in his maw.

Wormish and bewhiskered
like a catfish, noodling
his supple way through crannies
even spawn had found unreachable,
he survived solely
on what others could not use.
One day I discovered
that, like a cat, he had nine lives.
For days I had missed him
nosing pedantically
among the plastic ferns,
and guessed that he was dead,
eaten by some less pacific fish.

I cleaned the tank completely,
religiously, a sort of purging
and renewal after death—
sieved the gravel, scraped scum off the glass—
in short, remade the tank
with brand-new water, plants and fish.
Three days later he appeared again,

a ghost loach, returned as if to say
no world I created could exist
without the likes of him. I hardly
believed it, but there he was, oddly
glorious in resurrection,
and eating shit once again.

To a Fly Trapped in Amber

Our father
in his glowing amber cube is silent now,
a sullen candy
locked in resin like a jewel.
His kingdom
came and went. We are the sons he never knew.

You and I
settle roundly to our coffee cups and weep
for all the creatures
that have gone away, and for those that
still remain.
Blessed is the beast who dies in his right time.

Blessed too
the man who sifts through beach marl, squatting on his hams,
looking for sea shells
that will speak to him. If the same shell
held a man
up to its ear would it also hear the sea?

I believe
all the fossil things that ever swam or flew
are within us still
as voices crying from a deep and
poignant tomb.
This prayer is to say the dead things have not died

but live on
in thought, just as we live on in our own minds
like legends, awaiting
worlds to come—we whose glory is not
forever,
believing that our glory is forever.

Whistle Maker

> *. . . even in decline the people of Sian devised pleasures. They tied bamboo whistles of varying pitch to the tail feathers of pigeons so that when circling in hundreds overhead the birds made the sound of a flying pipe organ.*
>
> from *Stillwell and the American Experience in China* by Barbara Tuchman

The smoke from joss sticks in gray alleyways
paints characters into the wind—
phonetics, radicals—acrid brushstrokes
of supplication to an angry god.
In dark times, I have heard it said,
the deities demand perfume.
Down here, things grow more fetid by the hour.

Last night, outside of Sian's wall, a head
was found amid a stretch of peony,
drained of all blood, unrecognizable,
a present from the murderous *tu fei*.
Other signs—a cuckoo dying in mid-trill,
a nursing mother's teat gone dry, a swarm
of hornets blackening the lake—
have scared our citizens to death.
Everyone waits now for the sky to fall.

I say hold it up by any means—birds
and prayers if necessary, wooden flutes
and looks of wild surprise, hot bowls
of congee, turnips and the promise
of a song. If this is the end of time
I take it as my solemn task
to tame solemnity to tears, chasten
fear into a smile of wry acceptance
and put aside the coffins I must build.

I am master carver in this town,
but I make whistles now, of young bamboo
as thin as babies' bones. The beggar children
bring me pigeons they have trapped. I pay them
with sweet lucre—bits of candied rice.

And then I go to work. I stroke each bird
into a trance. I coo to them.
I whisper in their ears that they are air
and this so pleases them they swoon,
becoming soft and docile as I turn them
into something not quite bird
and not quite instrument of praise.

Slowly, the populace is catching on—
a shaman, busy prophecying doom,
is called from reverie by whisperings
of music thrown down from the sky;
in noodle parlors, old men debating
crops or politics pause with broth
and lo mein streaming down their chins to reap
the sound of wings out of the breeze;
a mother, staring at her child,
thinking there is no future here for him,
is stunned to laughter by a sudden cadence
tumbling from the stagnant summer air.

Soon the city talks of nothing else.
"The birds, the birds are coming back!" they cry,
and gather in the square to wait for them—
a feather-cloud that bursts into a rain
of music, droppings, and the laughter
of ten thousand Chinese, greater
than the history of our Sian,
the ancient dynasties of Han and T'ang
and all the lost magnificence
that we shall never see again.

And no one knows that I have done this thing.
It shall remain that way. I hope the gods
think my praise sweeter than perfume,
and I thank them for having been allowed
to make these wind instruments, thank them too
for having been an instrument of the wind.

Whistle Maker, by Robert J. Levy, received the 1986 Anhinga Prize for Poetry. The Anhinga Prize is awarded annually for a book-length manuscript of poetry in English. The winner is chosen in an open competition, and the final decision is made by a poet of distinguished achievement. For more information on Anhinga Press and the Anhinga Prize for Poetry, send a stamped envelope to Anhinga Press, P.O. Box 10423, Tallahassee, Florida 32302.

Winners of the Anhinga Prize for Poetry

Robert J. Levy, *Whistle Maker*, 1986
Judith Kitchen, *Perennials*, 1985
Sherry Rind, *The Hawk in the Back Yard*, 1984
Ricardo Pau-Llosa, *Sorting Metaphors*, 1983